YOUR REWARD SHALL NOT COME OF THIS EARTH

JOHN GLOEGE

ISBN 979-8-88943-784-0 (paperback)
ISBN 979-8-88943-786-4 (digital)

Christian Faith Publishing
832 Park Avenue
Meadville, PA 16335
www.christianfaithpublishing.com

All biblical quotations are taken from the New International Version (NIV) of the Holy Bible.

Printed in the United States of America

CONTENTS

ACKNOWLEDGMENTS

I was fortunate to have a wonderful upbringing and childhood. My parents, Dennis and Pat Gloege, provided much love and support to me and fully allowed me to pursue my goals and dreams. I couldn't have asked for better parents. My grandparents, Harvey and Loville Gloege, taught and instilled in me a Christian mindset from a very early age. My Christian values are largely from their teaching and example. My daughter, Mary, has been a tremendous blessing in my life from the moment of her birth. Our love for each other has brought us through some difficult situations. What a joy to have a close relationship with her! I believe one of life's greatest blessings is to have loving grandchildren. In my mind, I have the two best, Julia and Amy. Leaving behind a legacy for them and chronicling parts of my life were big reasons I decided to write this book. I want to bolster their belief in God and show them the importance of God in my life.

My life was transformed when I married my wife, Shirley, in 2015. I love her dearly, and she has been a wonderful helpmate assisting me in so many areas of my life. She has offered keen insight into some of the topics in this book. My darling Shirley has opened my eyes and ears to the Word of God through what the Bible says. Her strong faith in God and living from a standpoint of victory has had a tremendous influence on me.

My uncle, James Glaeg, an author himself, provided invaluable feedback into the writing of this book from an author's point of view. My friends, Steve Cartwright and Doug Patnode, provided good insight regarding the direction of the book. Princeton Branch

Librarian, Kathy Beck, provided valuable technology help during the writing of this book.

My biggest thanks as to the formation of this book goes to Tamika Cole, my stepdaughter, and Shannon Arens, my former teaching colleague and dear friend. Their insight, advice, and formatting were irreplaceable. They went over and above the call of duty to help me.

PREFACE

WRITING A BOOK AND LEAVING A LEGACY

What a thrill it is to realize I may be strengthening the faith of people by telling this story. *Helping others have a stronger belief in the existence of God is my main goal in writing this book.* It is so gratifying to know I'm doing something to please the Lord and grow His kingdom. What an honor!

Another great benefit to writing this book is to document my "eight-word experience" for the benefit of my relatives, friends, and especially my granddaughters. The document will serve as a living legacy long after I've departed from this life. So many times I've wondered what the best words would be to help Jesus come fully alive in my granddaughters' lives. This book will chronicle many of the things I want to convey to them to strengthen their faith.

My granddaughters are thirteen and eleven years old at the time of this writing. Those are young ages to fully understand Scripture and a lot of spiritual concepts. A person can get only to the surface when talking with them about many of the topics of this book—religion and spirituality. However, at some point in their lives, they will be at a better age to understand the points I am trying to make in this book. I'm praying that this book will help them realize that living to inherit eternal life is of ultimate importance to them. My hope is that some of the things I have written will leave a road map as to how to find eternal life and reinforce what they have already learned and will learn in the future about topics I've written about. Most importantly, I want my granddaughters to understand how important my relationship with the Lord is to me. In my view, helping children and grandchildren see one's faith and strong relationship with the Lord is the most important thing we can pass along to them.

This book will also help the girls know more about my life concerning important events that took place before they were born. They will have a general chronology of my life and will learn in greater detail about some of the things that have happened and some of the things I did in my life. I have an uncle who prepared a similar document for all interested parties on the lives of his mother and father, my grandparents. The document was based on many interviews he had with my grandparents over the years. My uncle's work covered important thoughts and events in each of his parent's life and was extremely interesting, informative, and valuable. I appreciated his work, and I learned a tremendous amount from his efforts. I gained very valuable insight into the lives of my grandparents. The document held extra special meaning to me due to the extremely close relationship I had with my grandparents.

I also look forward to sharing this book with many of my friends as well as other relatives. Spirituality, religion, and the Bible are not typically topics that are discussed in depth with friends or even relatives. I think this book will surprise some of my friends, and because we are more than casual acquaintances, I may have some credibility built up. When reading this book, my friends and relatives have knowledge of me, and because these people know me, they might be more likely to read the book to find out what I have to say.

Your reward shall not come of this earth.

CHAPTER 1

THE SUPERNATURAL EVENT

One warm Saturday, Autumn day in 1980, I was resting after a nice, home-cooked meal in the bed I had slept in since my ninth-grade year at Glenwood High School in Minnesota. The bedroom was upstairs in our three-bedroom house in which I had lived since I turned three years old. On this bright, sunny day, I was twenty-four years old and was just starting my second year of teaching at Princeton High School in Minnesota. I was so excited to be teaching and coaching three sports in the school district. Among the coaching assignments was the one I had dreamed about, head boys basketball coach. I was young, green, and excited to attempt building a great basketball program. I believe I was the youngest, large school class, head coach in the state.

I had been married a little over one year at that time. My wife at the time was also from Glenwood, so we both had roots there. We were both very close with our parents, which made for an easy decision to make the one-hundred-mile drive west from Princeton to Glenwood on the weekends, whenever we could. On this day, my wife was visiting her parents six blocks away while I was lying down to rest at about 2:00 p.m. My wife, Jean, grew up across the park from beautiful Lake Minnewaska, the thirteenth largest lake of Minnesota's 10,000. Her huge house was only a stone's throw from historic Lakeside Ballroom, which hosted a plethora of famous performers such as Louie Armstrong, Benny Goodman, The Andrew

Sisters, Vic Damone, and Fats Domino. That is just to name a few. Not bad for a sleepy, little, rural town of 2,500 people!

About five minutes after I lay down on my comfortable bed, a powerful, reverberating voice entered, not only my head but also my entire being. It was not an external, audible voice, instead an internal, booming voice that resonated through my entire body. The power of this voice caused my whole body to tingle. The voice sounded like thunder in my head, and the words echoed and rang inside me. The voice interrupted what I was thinking and came right on top of my thoughts.

The eight words that were revealed to me were: "Your reward shall not come of this earth." The words were very clear. My immediate thought was, What just happened? As I began to process this experience, I knew in my heart that this was a supernatural experience. The voice was unlike any I had ever heard. It was a very strong, deep, and masculine voice. It was not of this world. I knew it was God. The words were even biblical and old-fashioned, especially "shall not come of this earth."

I had never experienced anything like this. The event stunned me and left me with butterflies in my stomach, similar to the feelings a person might experience upon receiving very good or very bad, maybe life-changing news or similar to times in our lives that we are extremely nervous, maybe before an important competition. After I had a moment to process what had happened, my thoughts turned to *What does this mean? What is God conveying to me?*

The first thought that crossed my mind following these words was that I was going to have a difficult life. Up to that point in my life, I had some disappointing things happen to me, mainly related to the world of sports. As I will explain in chapter 3, "Heartache and a New Plan," I had an event in my life that was devastating to me. Were the eight words revealed to me related to the harrowing occurrence I experienced six years prior?

Sports had always been an extremely important part of my life. Almost all of my goals were related to athletics. I had some negative outcomes in important games and a few personal failures in key spots in big games. As head basketball coach at Princeton High School during my first year, the winter of 1979–1980, the team experienced some very tough, close losses. I began to entertain the idea that I may have been cursed in the area of sports. Something often seemed to happen to prevent me from reaching goals and gaining the happiness I was seeking from realizing accomplishments. I even wondered if God did not want me to reach these sports-related goals and attain the happiness and satisfaction that came with the accomplishments. Was I putting too much emphasis on sports in my life? Were sports an idol I was worshiping instead of God? Was I being overly prideful in wanting the glory that came with success in sports?

CHAPTER 2

SHARING MY EIGHT-WORD EXPERIENCE

When I experienced the revelation, "Your reward shall not come of this earth," one of the questions I asked myself was, should I share this encounter with anyone? I made the decision to keep the experience to myself. I'm not exactly sure why I decided to keep silent about the encounter. Now as I think back as to why I didn't talk about the experience, one of the main reasons was that I was not bold enough in my faith at that time in my life to unveil what many would view as controversial. I was afraid of what people would think of me if I talked about my episode. Would they think I had gone off the deep end? Was I afraid people would not want to associate with me anymore? Would people view me as some kind of religious extremist?

I think the answer to some of these questions, at least in part, is yes, I did fear what others may have thought. My spiritual maturity was not at a point where it has since grown to be. I didn't even tell my wife about the experience. I remember being fearful of how she might interpret the words revealed to me. Would she think I viewed our marriage as less than rewarding? The only person I shared the experience with at the time was my Aunt Linda. She was only seven years older than me, and I confided in her about everything. I held no secrets from Linda. In future years, I told my daughter, Mary, about the encounter. We are very close and have always had deep and personal conversations. I also discussed the revelation with my second wife, Shirley, and one of my brothers in very recent years. Those are the only people aware of my eight-word encounter with the Lord before writing this book.

I believe in our younger years, most people are very conscious and sensitive to how people view us. We want to fit into the mainstream and be thought of as normal by society's standards. We don't want to stand out as different or off the beaten path. We don't want to be considered weird. I believe talking about unseen happenings and things that can't be proven are often looked down upon. The supernatural and/or miracles are often doubted by a significant percentage of people. I think some people feel susceptible to feeling weak or gullible when admitting belief in supernatural events. For some reason, these vulnerable feelings can intensify when talking about spiritual topics. I believe many people are simply afraid of talking about their religious beliefs because of what people might think of them.

It has been my experience as I've grown older that I don't care near as much as I did in my younger years about how people view me. I am much more likely to express my feelings without worry with each year that passes by. I realize I am mortal, and I have already lived many more years than I have left to live. The prospect of people viewing me as different doesn't faze me. Therefore, it becomes easier and easier for me to share my love of God as time passes. To sum it up, I believe I have learned to live more for the eternal rather than the temporal.

After these many years since receiving the message, "Your reward shall not come of this earth," I have a much better understanding of the experience. I believe the words the Lord spoke to me have a double meaning. God was telling me there will be at least my share of disappointment and heartache on this earth. Life will not be one successful, happy event after another. There will be other people on earth who appear to attain everything they strive for. It may seem to me that everything these people touch turns to gold as the saying goes. However, at the same time, God was not telling me happiness and contentment would be unattainable in life, which was my original thought when the words resonated in me.

The second meaning of God's message to me is extremely exciting and gratifying. *By telling me my reward shall not come of this earth, the message is promising there will be a reward waiting for me in heaven.* This interpretation is so exhilarating and comforting. Now I need to live a life honoring God and pleasing to Him.

CHAPTER 3

HEARTACHE AND A NEW PLAN

Let's back up to November of 1974, my freshman year in college at St. Cloud State University. I was part of the St. Cloud State University basketball team on a partial scholarship. While doing a simple warm-up, layup drill two weeks into the season, I felt my heart suddenly begin to palpitate. Before I knew it, I came back to consciousness with concerned teammates and coaches closer to my face than I wanted, firing questions at me nonstop. As it turned out, I have a heart condition. It is a form of cardiomyopathy called hypertrophic cardiomyopathy, and the doctors ended my basketball career. I felt like my life was over, and I was devastated. Basketball had been my life. I had dedicated myself to becoming the best player I could possibly be, spending countless hours shooting baskets at the hoop attached to our garage since I was six years old. I had to pull myself out of a depression and reshape my goals. My life had been turned upside down.

I did the best I could to move on from the catastrophic event. I attended the basketball team's home games, and I socialized with friends as most college kids do. It was depressing and frustrating to have my love of basketball and goals of success in the game taken from me. Fortunately, I had a good support group of friends and a roommate who was my best friend.

Empty is one of the best words to describe how I was feeling. There was a huge void in my life, and I was having trouble making

7

sense of it all. An interesting, and somewhat humorous, story illustrates how I dealt with the immense frustration for one night. My roommate and two other friends went to the Press Bar in St. Cloud one cold January Saturday night to listen to live music and have a couple drinks.

The bar was jammed full of St. Cloud State University students at the popular establishment. Since the place was very crowded, we were forced to sit on the top floor of the double-deck layout. The band was very good, much to the delight of the big crowd gathered after a week of attending classes. Then the band started playing the song "Johnny B. Goode" written and performed by Chuck Berry.

Something hit me, and I started to dance at the table in which we were sitting. As I danced, I became fueled with a tremendous energy, and I felt the frustration inside me come bubbling to the forefront. My "frustration dance" became wilder and more of a spectacle with every few seconds that passed. After thirty seconds, I looked around and noticed the entire establishment watching me. Even the people on the dance floor were gazing up at me. Being my name is John, the incentive to egg me on was even greater for the group of friends I was with. At that point, I had no other choice but to keep on dancing until the song's completion.

When the words, "Your reward shall not come of this earth," were revealed to me six years later, in 1980, I thought God might be, in part, giving an explanation for the fainting episode that wiped away basketball, the most important thing in my life at that time. I felt God was telling me that basketball was not the ultimate reward or fulfillment I would receive.

As I have gone through the years, I have come to realize that the eight words God spoke to me— *"Your reward shall not come of this earth"—were actually a promise of ultimate happiness in eternal life*. At the same time, the words were not necessarily an indicator of unhappiness in this life. The Lord assured me that I have a reward coming in eternal life by saying my reward shall not come of this earth. If my reward doesn't come of this earth, it surely will come in heaven. What a joyful and assuring promise! Our reward in heaven will certainly exceed any reward this world could possibly offer. Therefore, it is still possible for me to live a happy, satisfying life on earth before gaining my ultimate reward in heaven.

After my basketball career ended, I changed my goals to being more service-minded. In His proclamation to me, God was promising me a reward in heaven. So one of my first challenges regarding God's message was balancing the realization that my reward would not occur in this lifetime with the elation of knowing I have a reward coming in the next life.

I have come to realize that I am blessed and favored in this life. I've had many great and unexpected things come my way in life. My wife, Shirley, has instilled this attitude in me and helped me realize I am blessed and favored. We were married in April of 2015, and the major part of my spiritual maturation parallels with that date. She frequently talks about herself being blessed and favored and often gives me examples of experiences in her life that back up her claim. I have learned we must recognize and declare that we are blessed and favored. *When we pray, we should pray as if what we are praying for has already been granted by God. If our request isn't already present, it is on its way. When we pray boldly, we are prophesizing our future.*

We should pray, not for victory in our lives, rather we should pray from a position of victory. We should pray from victory because the enemy has already been defeated by Christ dying on the cross for the forgiveness of our sins. Therefore, we are already victorious if we accept the gift of salvation.

You may ask, if I'm so favored, why all the disappointments in sports, removal of basketball in my life, and the early loss of loved ones? I believe the tough spots in sports and the ending of my basketball career was God keeping me humble and keeping me from idolizing sports. I now realize I was putting sports, particularly basketball, on a pedestal. The success I was having was making me too proud. The Bible indicates many times that God loves humility and disdains pride. God wanted more of my time and focus.

I have lived a very happy life. It has been very rewarding having the opportunity to impact many lives of young people through teaching and coaching. As an educator, I was never going to become monetarily rich, but I became rich in so much more of an important way. I'm not sure anything can be more rewarding than having former student/athletes tell me years later that I was a big influence in their lives.

Like all people, I had many disappointments and some heartaches to go along with the happiness I've experienced in life. In addition to missing out on my much-desired college basketball career as well as some disappointing outcomes in big spots in some important games, I have experienced at least my share of nonsports-related devastation. My first wife and I experienced the death of our first child at the age of two months due to a heart defect. Also, my first wife and I had a turbulent marriage that ended in divorce after nineteen years. In addition, my mother passed away at age fifty-two after a nineteen-year battle with cancer. My father died at age sixty-five, following a brief encounter with colon cancer.

However, in spite of a good deal of heartache, my interpretation of those eight words has evolved from a pessimistic message to a positive one. At about age sixty, I came to realize because of the eight words God spoke to me, a great reward awaits me in heaven. Until then, I can experience a happy life in this lifetime.

As the years are passing by in my adult life, I am realizing God has a plan for my life. I believe that is why He spared me at age eighteen, the day I fainted during college basketball practice, and at age sixteen, during physical education class, when an identical fainting episode occurred. It is not uncommon for sudden death to occur with the type of heart condition I have. Years ago, some deaths that happened on the basketball court went unexplained. University of Nevada, Las Vegas, basketball star Hank Gathers died on the court with this heart condition. More recently, with medical advances in cardiac testing and imagery, doctors have determined many of these types of deaths are linked to cardiomyopathy. Cardiomyopathy is an irregularity of the rhythm of the heart. Strenuous exercise can throw the heart out of rhythm, when someone has this condition.

I believe the Lord had plans for me to be a positive influence on many lives I came in contact with during my several years of being an educator and coach. I have always had a strong desire to help people, especially kids, feel good about themselves. I've always felt many of the mental health problems people have are caused by low self-esteem. My philosophy in working with people has been to build their self-image using a very positive approach when instructing them. I've tried to avoid, at almost all cost, putting students/athletes down when disciplining them.

C HAPTER 4

BASKETBALL ADDICTION
AND IDOLATRY

Going back to my childhood, high school days, and my first year of college, I now realize how important basketball was to me. I loved other sports too, but basketball held a special spot in my heart. One might say I was obsessed with the sport. To this day, I still have recurring dreams about playing in a high school or college basketball game with a good crowd in attendance. This experience of playing in front of a crowd and having the chance to show off the skills I had honed since being six years old sounded very thrilling to me. I loved the rush of adrenaline that flowed through me while competing in front of a big crowd.

The addiction I had for basketball started long before organized, competitive games, however. In fact, I can easily and honestly say the addiction started the first night my father took me to the small gym at Glenwood High School for his weekly shirts versus skins men's pickup game. The men decided to play half-court basketball that night. That left the other half of the gym open for me to shoot baskets. The ten-foot basket was a long way up in the air for a boy who hadn't yet reached his sixth birthday. It proved to be no problem once I figured out that I could get the ball to the basket if I hoisted it up with two hands in an underhanded fashion.

12

I quickly discovered I had a pretty good knack for putting the ball through the hoop. In fact, I was so thrilled with myself that I began to count the number of shots I made. I was in my glory when the school superintendent passed through the gym on his building walk-through. I knew the superintendent from church, and he was a good friend of my grandfather, therefore, I felt bold enough to yell out, "Hey, Mr. Carlson, I've made thirty-two baskets!" Mr. Carlson didn't seem overly impressed and probably wondered why my father had me out at nine on a school night, but I quickly learned that seeing a basketball I shot go through the net was an almost unparalleled thrill for me. There was something addicting about seeing that ball go through the net. Sometimes, the ball would go through the basket without touching the rim, swishing through the net. Other times, the ball might ring around the basket rim a few times before deciding to finally enter the net and go through. Every made basket seemed to be handled in a different way by the net.

I was on my way to a basketball addiction with as much compulsion as cigarettes are to a smoker or an alcoholic drink is to an alcoholic. This obsession for basketball only intensified as I started to gather acclaim for my basketball accomplishments in junior and senior high school.

Before I knew it, the time came for me to select a college to attend. I'm not proud to say that there was only one factor I weighed in selecting my college. You probably guessed it —basketball was the determining factor. Where was the best fit for me to continue my passion for basketball? I wanted to play at the highest level I could, and I wanted to be recruited, so I knew there was a reciprocal interest.

St. Cloud State University in central Minnesota was the perfect fit. St. Cloud was sixty-five miles east of my town of Glenwood, and I knew of many of the team members and had competed against some in high school basketball. The head basketball coach at SCSU, Noel Olson, had been recruiting me and even came to Glenwood to watch a game and have dinner at our house.

Everything seemed perfect. I even had the ideal roommate, Dave Moe. Dave was my best friend with whom I played basketball and baseball with in Glenwood. I was so excited about this new chapter in my life. I would be getting the opportunity to play in front of big crowds, get to know a new set of teammates, and represent the nice community of St. Cloud. Also, I must admit that the prospect of being well known on campus and the recognition and acclaim that would come from a successful college basketball career was enticing.

However, it all ended in a heartbeat (pun intended) on that October day in 1974, when I fainted during basketball practice. My life obsession was yanked away from me. My dreams were dashed in an instant, and everything I had been aiming for was taken out of focus. I had to reassess my life and totally change my goals. In a way, I had to change my reason for living. Basketball had been my life to that point, and I went into a depression. What was I going to do now? How could this have happened to me?

As the years have passed, a theory developed in my mind as to how God could let basketball be taken from me. The first commandment states, "Though shalt have no other gods before me." Had I turned basketball into a god? Was I taking away devotion I should have been giving to God, and, instead, putting basketball on a pedestal? I have come to the conclusion that the answer to these questions is yes. I had made basketball an idol. Basketball had taken on a position of too much importance in my life. An idol can be defined as the worship of someone or something other than God as though it were God.

God had to get my attention. Exodus 34–14 says, "For thou shalt worship no other god: for the Lord, whose name is jealous is a jealous God." I wasn't getting down on my knees and consciously worshipping basketball, but basketball was taking up a lot of space that I should have been giving to growing my relationship with God and glorifying Him. I believe God took basketball away from me so that I had more time and energy to serve Him. At that point in my life, God at least wanted me to acknowledge and pay attention to Him.

That service to Him started almost immediately when I saw a notice on the bulletin board outside the Halenbeck Hall Gymnasium, the arena where I would have played my college basketball games. The note was from a small parochial school in nearby Sartell, Minnesota. That school was looking for a volunteer to coach the grades 6–8 boys basketball team. I jumped on the opportunity and coached the team for three seasons as I took my college classes. I also found myself coaching football and baseball for the school. What a great way for a college student to get a coaching résumé started! In addition, doctors did allow me to play college baseball for St. Cloud State University in the spring, and that took a bit of the sting of not playing college basketball away. Baseball is a far less strenuous sport to play compared to basketball. Although not near the same for me as playing college basketball, the ability to compete and be a part of a team was very important to me for those four years of college. My plan, even before my basketball career ended, was to be a physical education teacher and coach basketball and baseball at the high school level.

So God started preparing me for my life's path without delay. The Lord knew I could touch more lives working with kids and helping them feel good about themselves than by being a good basketball player. Ideally, I would have wanted to both have a good college basketball career and become a teacher and coach at a high school. However, God had other plans for me. Maybe He wanted to keep me humble and hungry to succeed only through working with kids.

Over the years, as I worked with kids in class and coached them in sports, I came to realize I was doing the work God called me to do. I am one of the people to have been blessed to enjoy my work immensely. I found my work with kids to be stimulating and rewarding.

CHAPTER 5

PRIDE: "A THORN IN MY FLESH"

Along with me making basketball an idol in my life, I believe another reason God took basketball away from me was that success in basketball contributed to a prideful heart in me. I didn't realize it through my high school years, but I believe I let some of the accolades I had earned through basketball go to my head more than they should have. When a teenager is between the ages of fourteen to seventeen, it is easy to become impressed with oneself when told how good a basketball player you are. It is easy to develop a prideful attitude, subconsciously or consciously.

Although I thought I was very good at basketball, I have learned through the years that there is always someone better at something regardless of how skilled a person may be at something. We sometimes think we are about as good as anyone concerning a skill in any area in life, but someone always comes along to prove better at the skill or talent. An example I think of along these lines is every school seems to have a bully who intimidates his or her way to the top of the "most feared" list of the student population. Once in a while, another student will challenge the bully's prowess by engaging in a physical fight with the bully. If the challenger wins the fight, he or she will dethrone the bully as the "king of the hill," so to speak. Most of the time, the bully prevails to defend the title of the "toughest kid on the block."

However, the bully will ultimately meet his or her match and learn there is always someone tougher that can humble a person in a minute. A new student may move in to teach that lesson or the bully may meet his or her match in another town as time progresses. *It never benefits us to have an overabundance of pride, especially when we realize all our gifts and talents come from God. When we stop to think about it, all the good things and skills we have in our lives are gifts from God or other people. We have no reason to have too much pride about anything we possess or have accomplished.*

In 2 Corinthians chapter 12, Paul speaks of a thorn in his flesh. The Bible doesn't fully explain exactly what that thorn was. However, Paul gives a hint that at least, in part, the thorn may be related to pride. He says in verse 7, "Therefore, in order to keep me from becoming conceited, I was given a thorn in my flesh, a messenger of Satan, to torment me." The passage doesn't say the word pride, but the included word *conceited* is very closely related to pride.

Proverbs 6, starting with verse 16, lists things that the Lord hates. The first is a proud look. The others are a lying tongue, hands that shed innocent blood, a heart that devises wicked imaginations, feet that be swift in running to mischief, a false witness that speak lies, and he that sows discord among brethren. So pride is listed among what we think of as some of the worst possible sins we can commit. Make a note that pride is the first thing listed!

Thinking back to the time in my life when basketball was suddenly taken from me, I have come to the conclusion that pride was a thorn in my flesh. I didn't realize I was prideful during my youth and young adulthood, but pride was in my heart. I was polite and didn't wear the pride on my sleeve, but pride had crept into me through the success I had and what people said to me and about me.

In my mind, never overtly, one way this thorn in my flesh manifested itself is in the form of a jealous pride, an attitude developed in me that I had to be the best concerning all things related to athletics. If people bested me in some way related to sports, I had difficulty feeling happy for them. Instead, I had a tendency to feel jealousy that it wasn't me reaping the acclaim for the accomplishment. Whether I had been outperformed as a player, coach, or even as a sports official, I had to fight a temptation to feel resentful.

I have always felt ashamed of myself for this tendency of selfishness. I know it is wrong in God's eyes. I have worked at changing my attitude regarding the success of others my entire life. I can say that with God's help and a great deal of prayer, I have made great strides in being happy for the success of others. One telltale sign of spiritual maturity is when we start to care as much or more about others as we care about ourselves.

Between being prideful and making basketball an idol, I believe the Lord gave me a wake-up call the day he pulled basketball away from me through my fainting episode at St. Cloud State University basketball practice on that October day in 1974. He had plans for me that didn't include basketball to spread the Gospel through the many opportunities I had and still have during my lifetime. Although losing basketball was one of the most difficult things I have ever gone through, I now remember what God said to Paul when Paul asked God three times to take away the thorn in his flesh. The Lord said in 2 Corinthians 12:9, "My grace is sufficient for you."

God's grace has been more than sufficient for me to get through the heartache of having basketball taken out of my life when I was in college. The experience of losing basketball has given me a broader perspective of life and how things in life can so quickly change. The experience has shown me God is in control and causes me to reflect on Romans 8:28 which says, "And we know that in all things God works for the good of those who love Him, who have been called according to His purpose.

C HAPTER 6

——⬦——

THE WORKING YEARS

I had a good thirty-three-year career of teaching physical education, health education, and coaching various sports at Princeton Middle School and Princeton High School. In fact, as this book is being written, I'm still involved with coaching a high school sport. At age sixty-six, I am assistant girls and boys golf coach. Coaching golf is a totally different experience than most other sports. High school golf season provides a very relaxed atmosphere. The players' scores determine who will get the opportunity to compete in the interscholastic varsity matches. Therefore, there aren't a lot of tough decisions to be made as far as choosing who will compete in the high school golf contests. Because of the objective data provided by the golf scores, parental pressure on coaches is usually minimal. Also, golf is a non-contact sport and enables ample opportunity for social interaction with opponents.

It was an honor to have the opportunity to be a good role model for kids as a teacher and coach throughout my career. It was frustrating at times not to be able to overtly share my love for the Lord because of church-state separation laws. I know there has to be laws to "protect" people with different beliefs than Christianity or no belief in God at all. However, I feel children from Christian families could be reinforced in schools by countless teachable moments.

I did push the boundaries of my duties in one area, however. When I did my student teaching in Litchfield Minnesota the winter

19

of 1978–1979, I volunteered my services to be an assistant coach of the varsity boys basketball team. It was a great experience, and I learned a lot during my tenure in Litchfield.

The head coach at Litchfield was a Christian man by the name of Dave Buresh. One thing Coach Buresh did in his routine as coach was to lead the team in prayer before every game. That prayer time left a big impression on me as a young, aspiring coach.

When I accepted the job as head boys basketball coach in Princeton the following school year, I incorporated the same prayer practice before every game with every team I coached. I anticipated that some parent, at some point, might complain to administration that I was violating church-state laws. To my knowledge, nobody ever did lodge a complaint about the practice of prayer before games.

I am so glad I did establish the tradition of the pregame prayer. Teenagers need the reinforcement of Christian values in their formative years and to be exposed to the worship of God as often as possible. I had one player who was a senior at the time, tell me that he always stood next to me on my right side during the prayer before each game. The conversation with that former player indicated to me that the pregame prayer was significant to him and that he looked forward to the prayer each game.

I spoke recently to Coach Buresh and told him the positive impact he had on me as a coach. I mentioned to him that I was influenced in a positive way by his practice of praying before each game. Interestingly, he told me he started the pregame prayer because of the influence of a coach he assisted in one of his first basketball coaching assignments. Coach Buresh told me he was fortunate to work under a Christian man in the small town of Pipestone in southwestern Minnesota. The head coach at Pipestone led his team in prayer before each game, and that impacted Coach Buresh to pray with his teams. It is amazing to think how the Word of God travels from generation to generation in so many ways.

As I look back on the thirty-three years I taught and coached in the Princeton School District, I didn't often consciously reflect on the words spoken to me, "Your reward shall not come of this earth." Although I seemed to stuff the experience to the back of my mind as

I busily went through my working years, the eight-word experience was always with me. I always had the knowledge that God is real, in charge, and in total control of life. I could turn to the Lord in prayer, asking Him to be my Counselor and Provider. Knowing God is with me through the encounter I had with Him, I was able to go through my life with great confidence that the Lord is with me and in control of my life. I didn't need to worry. God is at the wheel, and He indicated to me that I have eternal life to look forward to. Nothing on this earth is important compared to the knowledge that there is a much better life ahead compared to life on earth. *The worst and most adverse times we can have in this lifetime don't come close to comparing with the joy that lies ahead in eternity.*

It wasn't until about age sixty that the eight-word experience came to the forefront of my mind. I started thinking about the encounter more and more. *Then, recently, I felt a calling to write a book about the experience to help others strengthen their faith and belief in the existence of God through my message from God.* The more frequent reflection on the encounter aligned with my relationship with the Lord becoming stronger.

Chapter 7

OUR MINISTRY

Now that I've retired from teaching and coaching, I realize there is another part to God's plan for me. That part of the plan is to serve the Lord and spread God's Word. I have been blessed to have many ways to serve the Lord. Many of these opportunities have come about as a result of my second wife Shirley's employment at Sterling Point, an assisted-living/memory-care facility in Princeton. She encouraged me to do a couple of things I never thought I would be involved in.

First there came a need at Sterling Point for someone to lead a Sunday church service in the chapel every second Sunday of the month. My very spiritual and outgoing wife volunteered the two of us to fill that monthly role. I have no formal training in theology, so it has been a growing experience. Shirley leads the prayer and musical portions of the service, while I deliver the sermon. Participation in the Sunday services has been such a faith-growing experience for me. It has brought me closer to God, and it has become evident to me that preaching the Lord's Word is a big part of His plan for me.

I have learned so much about God's Word by researching the Bible in preparation for my sermons. Along with the preparation, it has been so rewarding for me to interact with the approximately twenty-five residents who attend our services. I have so much enjoyed building relationships with the residents. The experience of researching and delivering sermons has significantly stretched me as a Christian. I have been forced out of my comfort zone to publicly deliver sermons to the residents.

Another source of spiritual growth for me has been leading a Bible study group, first at Sterling Point, then at Freemont Village in Zimmerman, Minnesota. One of the residents approached Shirley about the possibility of starting a Bible study at Sterling Point. Shirley asked me if I would consider conducting an every-other-week Bible study session with her. My thought was, *Let's give it a try*. Again, being the leader of the group was a big step out of my comfort zone. I would much rather be a group participant, instead of leading the group. As a result of my involvement in the ministry at Sterling Point and Freemont Village, I have grown and matured a great deal in my relationship with the Lord.

Shirley was right all along, when she told me that it was no coincidence we met on a Christian dating site. Our meeting was part of God's plan for us. We have work to do! We are to honor God's Great Commission to spread the Gospel to as many people as we can. *I heard a preacher who I greatly respect say that we all have one singular purpose in this lifetime when it comes right down to it. That purpose is to spread God's Word to as many people as we can to grow His kingdom.*

We have looked into and are considering conducting a prison ministry. What a great opportunity it would be to lead a ministry where many of the prison population are looking for a fresh start. Many are searching for something to believe in, and I'm also confident there is a significant percentage of inmates who feel undeserving of God's love and forgiveness. Teaching that Christ paid for their sins by death on the cross would be necessary. *The only requirements to gaining eternal life are proclaiming that Christ is Lord, Christ died for our salvation, confessing our sins, and accepting Jesus as our personal Savior.* The prison population seems like the perfect place to spread the Gospel.

Recently, I have come to believe writing this book is a part of God's plan for me to call people to Him. I enjoy writing, and I feel putting my thoughts on paper is a comfortable way to convey my thoughts. Writing allows me to organize my thoughts in an even more effective way than public speaking. It may have been fate for me to end up at St. Cloud State playing basketball for Coach Olson. He was a good man concerned about the well-being of his players. He followed proper protocol when I fainted during practice my first year at SCSU. He would not allow me to return to practice without medical clearance. Much to my dismay, that clearance never happened. I would have taken on any risk, no matter how severe, in order to play the sport I loved. Had I attended a different university, it is very possible a different coach would have allowed me to return to practice, shrugging off the fainting spell. Returning to practice could possibly have a tragic outcome sometime during my college basketball career.

Because of the words spoken to me, "Your reward shall not come of this earth," I feel compelled to share my testimony so others may more easily believe that God is real. I count myself very blessed to have this encounter with God. We all have moments of questions and doubts about our faith from time to time. Believing in the unseen is not always easy. It is normal for us to have doubts pertaining to our faith at times. If we are not experiencing some doubt, we are probably not thinking much about our faith.

How we deal with doubts and questions about the love, wisdom, and existence of God is extremely important. Talking with a mature Christian when experiencing doubt is always a good idea. Sometimes, a good conversation can bring our proper perspective back.

If we are feeling some doubt at times, we are in good company. On the cross, Jesus cried out, "My God, my God, why have you forsaken me?"

John the Baptist from prison sent his disciples to ask Jesus, "Are you the expected one?" John the Baptist seemed to be wondering, *If you are the expected one, why am I in prison?* There are things that can cause us to question the love, wisdom, and even existence of God. Perceived unanswered prayer and undeserved suffering are among topics that can cause doubts.

It is also wise to view our doubt as an opportunity to grow in our faith. Doubt should cause us to examine the sources of doubt through researching Scripture and healthy conversations with mature

Christians. Our faith can be made stronger by dealing properly with doubts that may creep in at times. *Above all, we must realize our doubts never diminish God's love for us. He is always there for us, even when we are not there for Him.*

CHAPTER 8

WHY DO BAD THINGS HAPPEN TO GOOD PEOPLE?

Why bad things happen to good people seems to be considered as one of life's great injustices. One of the first things we often think when we hear of tragedy to someone we know as a wonderful person is, *How could this happen to that person? He or she is one of the best people I know.* As long as this world will be in existence, there will be personal devastation and heartache. It can be very difficult for us to comprehend why personal destruction befalls even people of the greatest character at the most inopportune times. It just doesn't seem fair.

However, God never promised us paradise on earth during this lifetime. Instead, He indicated there will be tribulation in this life. John 16:33 says, "I have told you these things, so that in me you may have peace. In this world you will have trouble. But take heart! I have overcome the world." Although we will have troubles in this life, we can only imagine the paradise God has ready for us in heaven. Revelation 21:4 promises, "He will wipe every tear from their eyes. There will be no more death or mourning or crying or pain, for the old order of things has passed away."

Some people become very dismayed when terrible things happen to good people. It can be a real faith-shaker. We must remember that *this world is not the end.* It is very important for Christians to have an eternal perspective, rather than a temporal one. We have to stay focused on what lies ahead in eternal life, instead of letting the instability of this world dampen our spirit. Second Corinthians 4:17–18 tells us, "For our light and momentary troubles are achieving for us an eternal glory that far outweighs them all. So we fix our eyes not on what is seen, but on what is unseen, since what is seen is temporary, but what is unseen is eternal." It is very comforting to know a glorious reward awaits us in heaven.

Bad things definitely happen to good people, and to put it in perspective, the worst thing happened to the best person. The only righteous person to walk the earth was Jesus, yet He suffered more than we can imagine for forgiveness of our sins and to ensure our opportunity for salvation. God allows things to happen for a reason. We must remember that God is good, loving, and just whether or not we understand His motives. Instead of doubting His goodness, we need to trust God when bad things happen to us. Proverbs 3:5–6 says it best, "Trust in the Lord with all your heart and lean not on your own understanding; in all your ways submit to him, and He will make your paths straight."

In the Bible, Job is a tremendous example of bad things happening to a faithful servant of God. Job had every opportunity to turn away from God because of the terrible things He allowed Satan to do to Job. Job was faced with the appalling loss of his possessions, his children, and finally, his own health. What could be worse for Job? Yet he still refused to curse God. We do not always know why we suffer, but we can bring our pain and grief to God and trust in Him. Romans 8:28 states, "And we know that in all things God works for the good of those who love Him, who have been called according to His purpose." It is really hard to find "good" in tragedy to a loved one. It is inconceivable to think there can be anything positive in a devastating circumstance such as a death to a family member. That is where our faith must sustain us. Second Corinthians 5:7 commands us, "For we live by faith, not by sight." This Bible translation is from the New International Version (NIV). Other translations tell us to "walk by faith, not by sight."

One positive thing that can come from our suffering is that it may draw us closer to God. The "bad" can be devastating, but it can result in spiritual good. The way we grow in many areas of our life is through adversity. When facing devastation and heartbreak, we must emulate Job and continue to honor and glorify God.

God sometimes allows bad things to happen to show us we desperately need Him. Suffering can do one of two things: it can make us run away from God or it can draw us into a more intimate relationship with Him.

Another way to look at the question why bad things happen to good people is, "Why does God let good things happen to bad people?" Because we have all fallen short of deserving His glory. We are blessed and fortunate that Jesus died on the cross for forgiveness of our sins and our salvation.

Chapter 9

FAITH

For you to fully benefit from this book, you must believe my eight-word experience did actually happen. I can assure you this communication did occur. I would never misrepresent God in any way. He is the way, the truth, and the life. Since I began writing this book, I have started to realize that one of the main reasons God spoke to me on that warm, autumn day, years ago, was to plant the seed for me to write this book when the time was right. Well, the time is perfect now. At this stage of my life, I am retired from my career as teacher, coach, and sports official, giving me more time. Another reason the time is perfect to chronicle the eight-word experience is that I have grown in my relationship with the Lord exponentially in the forty-three years since the experience.

As we get older, I believe our relationship with God has ample opportunity to become stronger. Priorities in our lives have a chance to line up in a more godly way. We may not have the need to give our work career the attention it once needed as we retire or near retirement. Our children grow up and leave the nest as we reach a point in our lives, giving us less parenting responsibilities and more opportunity for reflective, quiet time. Spiritual maturity also has a better chance to take root as we grow older. If we are wise, we reflect on our lives, learn from our mistakes, and come to recognize and appreciate the many blessings we receive from the Lord. Finally, as we age, we start to realize our mortality. We know we have lived more years than we have left to live. This has a way of sobering us, helping us realize what is important in life. In a way, I think we come to the conclusion that we are all on the same team. Things we used to think important in life now seem small in magnitude. All the competing with people to get ahead or advance our standing in society or in our career seems unimportant as we reach a certain stage in life. Christians come to realize that we want the kind of relationship with the Lord that will gain us eternal life.

I heard about a ninety-plus-year-old man who was being interviewed and was asked what he had learned through his years of life. His response was, "Nothing is that important." His response was profound, especially if you are a Christian. It reminds me of scripture found in Matthew 6:34 that says, "Therefore do not worry about tomorrow, for tomorrow will worry about itself. Each day has enough trouble of its own." All the worry in the world is not going to gain us anything. Worry is just wasted energy. God has promised to provide for our every need. Matthew 6:26 states, "Look at the birds of the air; they do not sow or reap or store away in barns, and yet your heavenly Father feeds them. Are you not much more important than they?"

I believe the man was also implying nothing here on earth is worth getting stressed out about. Nothing compares in importance to what lies ahead in eternal life. We will be set totally free from all burdens. *Romans 8:18 says it this way, "I consider that our present sufferings are not worth comparing with the glory that will be revealed in us."*

So the elderly man being interviewed had the proper perspective on worry. It serves no benefit. As we grow older, it is easier for us to have this perspective on worry. We are more likely to be settled into and accepting of the quality of life we will have for the remainder of our lives, instead of worrying about our positions in our job, in society, and competing for better ways to provide for our families.

I enjoyed the elderly man's life perspective, in part, because it aligns with my perspective. Don't get me wrong. I worried as much as anyone through my working years. If I could go back, I would certainly not worry near as much if I knew how things would ultimately turn out. However, we don't have the luxury of knowing how things will turn out in the future. This is where faith comes in. Faith is believing in what we cannot see. Thankfully, faith is an ongoing process that can and should grow and change as we age.

Another profound statement that has significantly helped me with my perspective on life is the following: *"All that matters when we take our last breath on earth is our relationship with the Lord."* We can take no belongings from this world with us when we die. All the things we have accomplished in life won't gain us eternal life. It won't matter how many friends we had or how much money we made. It is only our relationship with the Lord that matters when we take our last breath because when we die, all that matters is that we inherit eternal life. Have we accepted Jesus Christ as our personal Savior by the time we breathe our last? Have we proclaimed Jesus is Lord? Have we confessed our sins to Him? Have we acknowledged that He died for the forgiveness of our sins and rose three days later? These are the things that guarantee us salvation. It is not enough to be the greatest friend in the world and help people in need through our lives. It is the confessing of sins, declaration that Jesus is Lord, recognizing He died and rose three days later for forgiveness of our sins, and accepting Him as our Savior that gives us eternal life. All the good works we do in this life are admirable and pleasing to God, but the Bible says in Ephesians 2:8, *"For it is by grace you have been saved, through faith—and this not from yourselves, it is the gift of God."* Salvation is not a goal to achieve, rather it is a gift to be received.

I believe the "by faith, not works" concept is one of the most undervalued and misunderstood biblical truths. The common belief seems to be if someone is so good to people and does many things to make the world a better place, how could God not let that person into heaven? God may answer that no one is a "good" person. Let me explain this controversial, potential response. There are many nice, friendly, helpful, and well-meaning people in the world. However, the only good person in the world is God. None of us are worthy of inheriting eternal life until we are born again of the Spirit. Romans 3:23 says, "For all have sinned and fall short of the glory of God." In addition, Luke 18:19 states, "Why do you call me good?" Jesus answered. "No one is good—except God alone."

Everyone is born into sin because of original sin. We are saved from the consequences of original sin by the grace of God through accepting Jesus as our Lord and Savior, believing that Jesus Christ died on the cross to redeem our sins, confessing our sins, and being baptized of the Spirit. Salvation is not based on our goodness but on Jesus's goodness. The Lord wants a personal relationship with us. He wants our attention and reverence. The faith, not works concept is difficult for many to comprehend. It is as if many people believe innate goodness is enough. This is one reason it is so important to know the Bible for yourself, instead of relying on the words and beliefs of others.

I can think of so many good people who I have come to know in my life who would do anything to help anyone. They are well liked and respected in the community. Many of these people I have gotten to know well enough to gain some insight into their spiritual beliefs. Since religion and spirituality are topics people typically avoid, it takes some time to have an idea as to a person's religious and spiritual views. Even then, we really can't be sure we accurately understand their relationship with the Lord. It is mysterious that most people go through life knowing so much about friends and acquaintances, yet so little about their religious and spiritual beliefs. These beliefs are usually deeply hidden inside of most people unless drawn out. Religious beliefs remain hidden because religion can be a forbidden topic of conversation. It can be an uncomfortable subject to discuss for many.

I have come to believe there are a lot of people in the world who believe in God but don't have an intimate personal relationship with Him. I believe many people have a relationship with the Lord that could be described as "lukewarm." It is not a wholehearted relationship. The relationship in many cases is only one of convenience. Many people will worship the Lord only when it is convenient for them. Many only worship or even acknowledge God when things are going well in their lives or when they have a need for God to meet. Some people only pray to ask the Lord for something and not thank, glorify, and honor Him. The first and great commandment found in Matthew 22:37 says, "Love the Lord your God with all your heart and with all your soul and with all thy mind."

We have to be all-in regarding our relationship with the Lord. We should not have a casual relationship with Him. Revelation 3:15–16 says, "I know your deeds, that you are neither cold nor hot.

I wish that you were either one or the other! So, because you are lukewarm—neither hot nor cold—I am about to spit you out of my mouth." The Lord wants us to be fully committed to Him.

What are the reasons for the lack of commitment to God on the part of so many people? That is the million-dollar question. I believe one reason is a lack of exposure to the Lord in many people's upbringing. Many youngsters are brought up without the encouragement or support to worship the Lord. Conversely, some people pull away from the pressure of parents to attend Sunday school and church, when they gain independence. I've heard many people express that they are "turned off" by what they perceive as hypocrisy on the part of churchgoers. At times, there is a perception of churchgoers acting "high and mighty" in church, then living a less than Christian life on the outside of church. It is good to remember that our public worship experience is about our personal relationship with God and is not dependent on other people's motives or relationships with the Lord.

There is a significant percentage of people who question, doubt, or deny the existence of God. This doubt about God being real is a key reason in my decision to write this book. I believe many people haven't taken the time to read the Bible and understand what the Lord requires of us to gain eternal life. All we need to do is declare Jesus is Lord, accept Jesus as our personal Savior, confess our sins, and believe in our hearts that Jesus died on the cross and rose three days later. *I fear many good, friendly, and helpful people may not go far enough in establishing a personal relationship with the Lord and are putting their eternal inheritance at risk. It is vital for us to get into our Bibles and learn the Word of God.*

One of Satan's favorite tools is to deceive people that there is a lot of time to confess our sins and accept Jesus. Satan would have us believe there is no hurry to ensure our salvation, and we have our whole lives to get around to being saved. However, we don't know when our lives will come to an end. It may seem like we have years to live, but even tomorrow is not promised. We must live prepared and have our lives in order. *To put it simply, we must live as though Jesus will return tomorrow.* We can't let the enemy deceive us into thinking that we have all the time in the world to get right with Jesus.

CHAPTER 10

SPIRITUAL GIFTS

First Corinthians chapter 12 tells us every believer will receive at least one spiritual gift during their Christian walk. Spiritual gifts are blessings or abilities given by God to His children through the power of the Holy Spirit. Many of the spiritual gifts talked about in the Bible are found in Romans 12:6–7, 1 Corinthians 12:8–10, 28–30, and Ephesians 4:11. Most of the spiritual gifts are centered around service to others.

The two spiritual gifts that are foremost in my mind, when I think about my spiritual gifts, are teaching and encouraging. These two gifts served me very well in my career as an educator and coach. I very much enjoyed my teaching and coaching career. I loved working with kids and still find myself in environments that I'm teaching, whether it be on the golf course or at an assisted-living facility.

My biggest satisfaction was helping kids feel better about themselves. It has been said that many people don't remember what they learned from the most impactful teacher they ever had, but they do remember how that teacher made them feel. I believe that is a very true statement, and I made making kids feel good about themselves my number one priority, when working with kids. I know of one teacher who when asked what subject he taught would answer, "I teach kids." If a person thinks back on the most impactful teacher in their school days, many times, it is the connection that developed between teacher and student that left a lasting imprint. As the saying goes, "Students don't care how much you know until they know how much you care."

So much of the school experience is the social learning that takes place between students and also between teacher and student. Students are in a position where interaction with an adult other than parents is required. Effective educators have the ability to help students develop and mature as individuals, and that is what it is all about. Children are fragile, impressionable, and need positive support from adults.

The second spiritual gift I have been blessed with is closely related to the gift of teacher. I am a natural encourager. I believe encouraging others is a good relationship builder. We all need to be encouraged in our lives at times, and we seldom know the impact an encouraging word or compliment will make in someone's life. I have learned I don't have to make an effort to be an encourager. It comes natural for me. It is a spiritual gift I have been blessed with.

It is amazing to me how far a simple compliment will go in making someone's day. For example, telling someone who just got a haircut or is sporting a new hairstyle that you like the haircut can really brighten their day. The person who got the haircut may have been self-conscious about how the haircut looked, and a simple compliment can put them at ease and put a pep in their step for the rest of the day. Giving a compliment or encouraging a person in some way is such an easy thing to do and can make a person feel good about themselves. The opportunity to encourage people comes along so frequently in a day. We have so many chances to brighten someone's day by a compliment or encouraging word. It has always puzzled me how underutilized the tools of encouragement are used in our society.

It is interesting how our spiritual gifts are sometimes released when we least expect it. I came to realize, as the years passed, that my true mission from God was not to build state championship teams in basketball and baseball but to build the self-esteem of early teenage kids looking for their identity in life, especially those who were not the most popular among their peers. I thought I got into teaching to be a highly successful coach. I had my share of both success and disappointment as a coach. I was head boys basketball coach at Princeton High School from 1979–1994. I resigned because of the rigors of the job. The effort I put into the job caused me to burn out. In the years that followed, I had more energy to put into my 7:30 a.m. to 3:30 p.m. teaching assignment. I gradually realized my assignment from God was to nurture and support the kids who needed a little extra attention and bolster their self-esteem. I found my spiritual gifs of teacher and encourager to be extremely beneficial in my efforts to make kids feel good about themselves.

Each of us has the ability to make the world a better place by reflecting on the spiritual gifts listed in Romans 12:6–7, 1 Corinthians 12:8–10, 28–30, and Ephesians 4:11. Self-examination and reflection can help determine the spiritual gifts that you have been blessed with. Recognizing and maximizing these gifts will be very pleasing to God and show others a glimpse of Him through us. By discovering our spiritual gifts and using them to fulfill the destiny God has for us, we are more easily and effectively able to do the work God wants us to do here on earth.

C HAPTER 11

ETERNAL REWARDS

I remember, when I was about age thirty, wondering if there are different "levels" in heaven according to the kind of life a person lived on earth. Is heaven the same for everyone? Or are people who live a more godlike life on earth rewarded with a better version of heaven compared to a person who is saved but lived a much less holy life? The Bible tells us we are given rewards in heaven for the life we live on earth. Revelation 22:12 says, "Look, I am coming soon! My reward is with me, and I will give to each person according to what they have done." The godlier life we live on earth, the more rewards we receive in heaven. These good works we do on earth do not earn our salvation. Ephesians 2:8–9 says we are saved by grace through faith in Christ Jesus and not by our own efforts or works. However, once we do gain salvation by accepting Jesus as our Savior and confessing our sins, we do store up treasure through good works we do in this lifetime. James 2:17 says, "In the same way, faith by itself, if it is not accompanied by action is dead." Although we are not *saved* by good works, we are expected to demonstrate our faith through good works.

Second Corinthians 5:10 says God will give rewards in heaven at the judgment seat of Christ, based on our faithfulness in service to Him. "For we must all appear before the judgment seat of Christ so that each of us may receive what is due us for the things done while in the body, whether good or bad." The law of sowing and reaping is also fulfilled by the granting of rewards. These heavenly rewards will be with us for eternity and are the completion of our earthly story.

I have thought often about and replayed in my mind the words: "Your reward shall not come of this earth." The words that once caused me some concern and uncertainty have become a source of comfort for me. *These eight words communicated to me on that beautiful, autumn day in 1980 are concrete proof that there is indeed a God, and He is watching over me and in total control of my life.*

Had my eight-word message not occurred, I know I would still have strong faith that there is a God. It has never been difficult for me to believe there is a God who created everything in this world. Also, I believe the Bible is inspired by God and that He gave His only Son for the salvation of all who accept this gift. However, being blessed enough to hear directly from God through this experience definitely snuffs out any doubt I may have previously entertained about God's existence without the encounter. I didn't realize it for many years, but I now believe God was planting a seed in me through this eight-word revelation to do my part to fulfill the Great Commission to spread the Gospel throughout the world. I'm actually spreading the Gospel of Jesus as well as helping anyone who will read this book more easily believe in the existence of God. Helping other people know in their hearts that God is real and in our midst is of utmost importance to me.

I should have been spreading the word about my eight-word message from God, when I first heard it and throughout the years that followed, and I should have been celebrating and talking to my friends and relatives about it. I believe one reason I was hesitant to share the experience with others until about age sixty is that I felt it was taboo to talk about God and religion with others. You know the saying, "Never talk about religion and politics"?

When the encounter with God occurred, and for many years after, I was immature in my faith. Now, although I have a long way to go, I am much more advanced in my understanding of the Lord. I'm now hoping everyone who reads the book will be strengthened in faith.

CHAPTER 12

WITNESSING DEATH

I had the unique experience for someone not in the healthcare field to witness four of my loved ones take their last breath of life. They are my mother, my father, my oldest daughter, and my first wife. None of their deaths were unexpected. My mother and father both died from cancer under hospice care. Jillian, my first daughter, was born prematurely and died after only two months of life. My first wife, Jean, died after being in a diabetes-related coma for about three days. We were divorced at the time of her death.

I was in the room with all four of these loved ones, along with other relatives as they took their last breath. I was actually observing their breathing when their chests stopped rising and falling. What are the odds I would literally witness their very last breath?

If I had it to do over again, I would have ministered to my mother and father as they were spending their last weeks at home under the care of hospice. As I previously mentioned, I was not in the same place spiritually as I am now. If I would have been a more mature Christian, I would have prayed with them and helped make sure they were right with God.

I certainly believe my mother, my father, Jean, and Jillian are in heaven. Jillian, of course, was only two months old. The other three were God-fearing Christians who believed in God. John 3:16 says, "For God so loved the world that he gave His one and only Son, that whoever believes in Him shall not perish but have eternal life."

In addition, Romans 10:9 says, "If you declare with your mouth, 'Jesus is Lord,' and believe in your heart that God raised Him from the dead, you will be saved." Note that in Romans 10:9, there is an extra requirement in gaining eternal life other than just believing in God. That requirement is declaring "Jesus is Lord." Many preachers add confessing your sins and also asking Jesus to come into your heart and to make Him your Lord and Savior.

The Romans 10:9 verse is often referred to as the Sinner's Prayer and constitutes being "born again" in many people's viewpoint. No matter what a person believes is required to attain eternal life, it certainly doesn't hurt to do everything the Bible suggests.

I would have enjoyed praying as well as sharing and discussing Bible scripture with my mother and father. However, I was not at that point in my spiritual journey. What a blessing it would have been to pray with the two people most responsible for my protection, nurturing, and loving care growing up.

We should not be timid regarding opportunities to share the Word of God with others, no matter if the witnessing is to relatives, friends, or even people we don't know, when the chance to do so arises. Rather, we should develop a boldness to seize the opportunity to fulfill God's Great Commission to spread the Gospel and grow His kingdom.

CHAPTER 13

❖

BORN AGAIN

The topic of being born again is an interesting concept to me. I grew up a Methodist and had grandparents who made sure I attended Sunday school regularly and, often, the following Sunday church service with them from the age of about five. I don't ever recall hearing the phrase born again relating to religion. The belief of the Catholic church and some Protestant churches seemed to be that baptism constituted being born again. Most of the baptisms happened before the child's first birthday. Some would argue that age is too early since the child is not yet at an age to make a conscious decision to accept the Lord as personal Savior.

I once asked a Catholic priest how he reconciled the concept of a young infant being saved through baptism without the cognitive ability to discern the meaning of the event. The priest responded that it was the responsibility of the parents to make sure the ceremony of baptism occurred. The belief of his church, along with many denominations, is that the ceremony of baptism is being born again.

When I was married the first time, I converted to Catholicism. In my years of being Catholic, similar to my Methodist upbringing, I don't recall hearing teaching on being born again. Therefore, I knew very little about what being born again meant or what constituted being born again.

After Shirley and I were married in 2015, we worshipped in the Catholic church, along with attending a nondenominational church sometimes. We greatly enjoyed the teaching at the nondenominational church and have settled into regular attendance at that church. The concept of being born again through declaring Jesus is Lord, confession of sins, acknowledging Jesus died and rose three days later for remission of our sins, asking Jesus to come into our hearts, and making Him our Lord and Savior, has been a consistent teaching at that nondenominational church.

So I have only been exposed to being born again the past eight years of my life. There appears to be a discrepancy of what is required to gain eternal life. The Catholic Church and some of the Protestant churches teach that baptism, even at an early age, constitutes being born again while churches such as Evangelical Christian, Pentecostal, Baptist, and many nondenominational churches believe declaring Christ is Lord, confession of sins, believing Christ died and rose again, and accepting Christ as personal Savior are required. Today's society tends to put a lot of emphasis on different church denominations. However, I'm certain God would tell us there are no denominations, and that we are all one family of Christians without the need for any other denominational designation.

Let's look and see what the Bible says about being born again. John 3 commands we must be born again of the Spirit. Specifically, John 3:5–6 says, "Very truly I tell you, no one can enter the kingdom of God unless they are born of water and the Spirit. Flesh gives birth to flesh, but the Spirit gives birth to spirit." Here, the word *Spirit* refers to the Holy Spirit. Of course, we can't return to our mother's womb to be reborn, so how is it that we are to be born a second time? *Born again* is in reference to the moment of faith and repentance. It is a spiritual rebirth. There is a communion between God's Spirit and our spirit. First Corinthians 3:16 presents the concept this way: "Don't you know that you yourselves are God's temple and that God's Spirit dwells in your midst?"

Preachers of Evangelical churches often like to close their sermons by offering their audiences an opportunity to pray the Sinner's Prayer (also called the Consecration Prayer and Salvation Prayer). This prayer involves any prayer of repentance prayed by individuals who feel sin in their lives and have the desire to form or renew a personal relationship with God through Jesus Christ. It is as simple as confessing one's sins, declaring Jesus is Lord, believing Jesus died and rose again, and asking Him to come into your heart, and making Him your Lord and Savior.

The sincere expression of this Sinner's Prayer is what constitutes being born again in Evangelical Christian belief. Romans 10:9 stresses the importance of confessing with your mouth, when it states, "If you declare with your mouth, 'Jesus is Lord' and believe in your heart that God raised Him from the dead, you will be saved."

I'm not here to judge what the Lord requires for us to inherit eternal life. John 3:16 indicates that believing in the Lord is the requirement for eternal life, while Romans 10:9 asks that we declare with our mouth that Jesus is Lord and believe in our heart that God raised Him from the dead so salvation will be ours.

Only God knows exactly what is required of us to inherit eternal life. It is interesting to note what Matthew 7:13–14 says about the narrow and wide gates:

> Enter through the narrow gate. For wide
> is the gate and broad is the road that leads to
> destruction, and many enter through it. But
> small is the gate and narrow the road that leads
> to life, and only a few find it.

This passage seems to indicate that less than half of the people who are born will gain eternal life when you compare the words "many will enter the wide gate" with "few will find the road that leads to life." The thought that few will find the road that leads to life should be very concerning to those who don't have a strong relationship with the Lord.

Going to church does not make a person a Christian. How we live our lives and the relationship we develop with the Lord are much stronger indicators of Christianity. However, there seems to be a significant percentage of people who don't attend church services regularly or even semiregularly. Lack of church attendance does not mean a person can't have a strong personal relationship with the Lord, but it would seem more difficult to nurture and grow that relationship. I am surprised at the number of people I perceive as nonchurchgoers. Even as I think of some people I know who I consider great people, I often am puzzled at their noncommitment to church. It seems as though they lack an urgency to grow their relationship with God. I believe not being brought up in a home that taught about the Word of God is a reason many seem to lack the passion to be in an environment to help grow their faith. Also, I believe some people lack the ability to believe in what they cannot see, which is what defines faith.

CHAPTER 14

RESURRECTION AND JUDGMENT

Along with providing proof to me that God does exist, the eight-word revelation, "Your reward shall not come of this earth," contains another important truth. The message implies there is a heaven. That also means there will be a resurrection. The eight words spoken to me reveal a great deal. First, God promises a reward is coming to me. Next, the reward won't be of this earth (this lifetime). If the reward isn't coming in this life, it will be coming in the next life (heaven). If I am to receive the reward in the next life, there has to be a resurrection. That resurrection of the body will happen to all people, believers and unbelievers. All people will be raised physically from the dead on the last day. The difference is that Christians will be raised to everlasting glory, while those who do not believe in Christ will be raised to judgment. Therefore, the resurrection will assuredly be a real occurrence. The believers "in Christ" will be resurrected, just as Jesus was resurrected. If there were no resurrection, who would Christ reign over for eternity?

Another important aspect of the phrase "in Christ" to consider is found in 1 Corinthians 15:22. It says, "For as in Adam all die, so in Christ all will be made alive." When we die, we don't automatically go to heaven. We must die in Christ and accept His free gift of salvation. To be in Christ is to believe Jesus Christ, the Son of God, who

45

was born in the manger, died on the cross, rose from the dead, and lives by His Spirit in the soul of every Christian believer.

The Bible speaks of two judgments—one for believers, the other for unbelievers. The judgment for believers is called the Judgment Seat of Christ. Believers will give an account of themselves to Christ. Second Corinthians 5:10 says, "For, we must all appear before the judgment seat of Christ, so that each of us may receive what is due us for the things done while in the body, whether good or bad."

Keep in mind the Judgment Seat of Christ does not determine our salvation. Christ already ensured our salvation by dying on the cross for forgiveness of our sins. However, we need to acknowledge Christ's sacrifice for us by proclaiming He is Lord and accepting Him as our Savior. The Judgment Seat of Christ is about rewards for our works in this life. Rewards are given and some withheld according to what we did for Jesus. You might say, "Where you spend your eternity depends on what you believe. How you spend your eternity depends on the way you live."

The Great White Throne Judgment, described in Revelation 20:11–15, is for the unbelievers in which they are judged according to their works and sentenced to everlasting punishment in the lake of fire. The Great White Throne Judgment is also known as the Final Judgment, and it will put an end to God's plan for this earth. This judgment follows the Millennium, God's one-thousand-year-reign on earth. No chance of a change of heart or belief after the Great White Throne Judgment is mentioned in the Bible. Eternity begins after the Great White Throne Judgment.

Chapter 15

BE READY

For generations, people have wondered when Jesus will return and questioned why He has not already come back. The fact that Jesus has not already returned is a source of doubt about the existence of Jesus for some.

We must remember what Matthew 24:14 reveals: "And this Gospel of the Kingdom will be preached in the whole world as a testimony to all nations, and then the end will come." The Gospel is the good news about Jesus's death and resurrection. This doesn't mean that every person will hear the Gospel, rather that every group of people will.

As the years have passed, and I have matured as a Christian, I have a much better understanding of the scripture found in Romans 8:28, And we know that in all things God works for the good of those who love Him, who have been called according to His purpose. So many things that have happened in my life seemed like a disappointment at the time. As I now look back, I can see how the events fit into God's will and plan for my life. God's plan for us may not be for us to understand at the time of events in our lives or maybe ever during our lives on earth. As the saying goes, God is playing chess while we are playing checkers.

God calls us to spread the Gospel and help others believe in Him. By writing this book, I am attempting to help all who read it to be sure in their belief in God's existence. The first and great commandment tells us, "Love the Lord your God with all your heart and with all your soul and all your mind."

I'm so thankful God spoke to me the words, "Your reward shall not come of this earth." Whenever my faith starts to weaken, I can come back to my encounter with God. It is evidence, I would imagine, not many people have the opportunity to experience. It is my prayer that those who read this book will have increased confidence that the Lord God Almighty exists and is in control of our lives. It is important we are right with God and have done everything we need to do to ensure salvation.

I hope I have not sounded arrogant in some of the things I have written in this book. If I am sounding overly privileged, it is a privilege available to us all. We simply need to be open to God's Word, establish a relationship with Him, and let Him be Lord of our life. *We need to be "in God" and "God in us" as we live our lives. All we need to do is accept God's free gift of salvation in order to realize His promise of our resurrection and to live together with Him for eternity.*

I feel so blessed to have experienced this eight-word revelation: "Your reward shall not come of this earth." I'm not proud that I have suppressed this communication from God for so many years. It took me a long time to mature spiritually and comprehend my calling to share this message.

Luke 12:48 implies that we are held responsible for what we have. The second sentence of the verse reads, "From everyone who has been given much, much will be demanded; and from the one who has been entrusted with much, much more will be asked." If we have been blessed with talents, wealth, knowledge, time, and the like, we are expected to benefit others with these gifts. I must fulfill scripture and honor God by revealing the words spoken to me, "Your reward shall not come of this earth."

I pray that reading this book will have been a faith building experience for you, and I hope you get as much out of reading the book as I have by writing it. God is real and is in total control of our lives, along with all that happens on earth. *We must not forget the vital reality that all that matters when we take our last breath on earth is our relationship with the Lord.*

The words revealed to me on that autumn day in 1980, "Your reward shall not come of this earth," have been a source of comfort, assurance, and joy for me. In reading this book, I hope you have gained confidence in the existence of God and in the reality that eternal life awaits believers in Jesus Christ.

Epilogue

One thing I have learned in life is success or failure in certain types of situations can become a self-fulfilling prophecy based on outcomes of similar situations in our past. Our mental expectation about how we will handle a situation in life is of vital importance in the outcome of the situation. The impact our attitude and expectations can have in determining the outcome of a situation is far undersold. Many times, the outcome comes down to whether you think you can or think you can't; you are right. To a degree, life is a self-fulfilling prophecy. Our attitude and expectations go a long way in determining outcomes of circumstances. Past outcomes in similar situations we have faced is a huge determining factor in the results of dilemmas we come across. Memories and results of past critical situations in our lives are deeply etched in our subconscious. We even remember how our body felt in those circumstances.

I was listening to a radio broadcast of an NFL football game recently. The game was to be decided by a field goal attempt with only a few seconds left on the clock. The pressure was on the kicker who was to attempt the field goal. If he makes the kick, his team wins the game. However, if he misses, all his team's effort to get to the position to win the game would go to waste. It is ironic that the huge, muscular, and athletic gladiators from both teams battle tooth and nail throughout the entire game only to have the outcome decided by a kicker, someone who only kicks for the team and seldom even has contact with another player.

The radio announcers were talking about the enormity of the kick. The kicker to attempt the game winner was a first-year player who was having an exceptional season. The color man of the broadcasting duo said, "He will make the kick. He doesn't have any scars yet."

I thought that was a very profound statement. As we go through life, we accumulate "scars," which we could describe as disappointments in life situations. These disappointments happen to all of us. How we handle adversity goes a long way determining how successful and happy we are in life. If we dwell on failures and disappointments we experience in life, we are more likely to fail when confronted with a similar challenge in the future.

The announcer was implying that if the kicker had missed some important kicks previously during the season, the kick would be more difficult to make because of memories of not coming through in similar situations. Failing to succeed in a situation important to us can leave a scar that can affect future, similar situations.

In reference to how we handle adversity relating to how successful and happy we are in life, I now realize that dwelling on past failures and disappointments has been a roadblock in my life. I look back too much on disappointing events in my life and think about my failure in certain situations. This negative reflection is very counterproductive relating to happiness and success in my life. Instead, I should learn what I can from the experience and move on from them. I have learned that I must "look ahead" in life, anticipating good things and what the Lord wants me to accomplish in the rest of my days. Reflecting negatively on past disappointments and failures is baggage that can prevent me from the success and happiness God has planned for me.

I have learned through heavy involvement in athletics that sports has a way of imitating life. There are so many life lessons that can be learned from the academic playground of sports. However, it is not only sports that can teach about life, but any form of competition or participation available to us. I believe all forms of extracurricular activities available in schools offer an outstanding platform to learn lessons that cannot be learned in the classroom. Schools offer band, choir, debate, drama, academic bowl contests, and many more opportunities. All of these programs offer students a chance to grow in all areas of life.

As far as sports, the ultimate mental game is golf. I have enjoyed playing golf since I was six years old. Golf is the only sport I still play actively. I love the sport and play many times a year. A few years ago, I noticed a pattern. I would have a very good game going, but I would find a way to ruin the game in the last couple holes. I would hit an uncharacteristically bad shot or miss a putt I would usually make. All of a sudden, I had a bad score or two on my scorecard to foul up an otherwise outstanding game.

The common thread in failing to come through in situations such as these was muscle tension. I wanted to succeed so badly that I tried too hard. Like most people, when I try too hard, the effort becomes counterproductive. Instead of performing athletically with relaxed muscles, tension in the muscles will almost always cause less than peak performance.

To counter my poor finishes on the golf course, I decided to try self-affirmation. Self-affirmation is convincing oneself that he or she is good in some skill or area of life. It could be affirming you have certain characteristics or are good at a certain life skill or phys-ical skill. Brainwashing one's self in a positive way is another way to describe self-affirmation.

In the case of making an effort to finish off golf games more effectively, I told myself each night, through meditation, that I was a strong finisher. I imagined myself hitting good shots and good putts on the last few holes of a golf game. I told myself I was totally relaxed and in charge of my thoughts and emotions as I played the last few holes. I used self-talk to convince myself I could finish off a game of golf as well as anyone. I told myself I get stronger as the game goes along and especially perform at my best the last few holes.

After using this self-affirming technique for about two months, I experienced outstanding results on the golf course. I performed much more effectively on the last few holes, both of good games and less than stellar games. I noticed more self-confidence playing the last few holes of a game. I felt more in control of my mind and my body.

I felt like I had overcome a mental obstacle because of self-affirmation. I feel self-affirmation can be an effective antidote, for anyone who believes it will work, to the mental block that can develop pertaining to failing in certain situations.

I'm writing about self-affirmation because it can be used in any area of life. By using concentrated self-talk, we can improve most any aspect of our life. It can help us be a better family member, a better friend, it can even help us be a more decisive person. Most importantly, self-affirmation can help us grow as a Christian. For example, we can use self-affirmation to declare we have strong faith. We can declare that we look forward to serving other people and that we are growing as a Christian all the time.

Philippians 4:13 is the optimum self-affirmation the Bible provides, and it says, "I can do all this through Him who gives me strength." This passage is the father of all self-affirmation. The verse says we can do all things through Christ. So other affirmations are just specific affirmations born of the declaration that all things are achievable if they are requested through Christ. We can self-affirm anything if we recruit the assistance of Christ. Christians have a huge advantage when it comes to self-affirmation because Christ is working on our behalf to imbed the affirmation into us.

Self-affirmation is a very underutilized and unexplored self-help technique. I have learned of its value firsthand in a few different areas of life. People use so very little of the potential the mind offers. I encourage you to explore the fruits self-affirmation can yield in your life and especially in building your relationship with the Lord.

About the Author

John Gloege graduated from Glenwood High School in Glenwood, Minnesota, in 1974. He was very active in athletics at Glenwood High School, participating in football, basketball, baseball, golf, and track. John went on to earn his undergraduate degree in physical education, health education, driver's education, and coaching at St. Cloud State University in 1979. John played college baseball at SCSU for four years. He received his master's degree in curriculum and instruction from the University of St. Thomas in 1985. John taught in the Princeton School District in Minnesota for thirty-three years, spending all but six of his years at the middle-school level.

He served as head boys basketball coach for fifteen years, coached Legion Baseball for nineteen summers, and is still currently serving as assistant boys and girls high school golf coach. After the majority of his coaching was completed, John embarked on a twenty-five-year basketball, football, and volleyball officiating career. John has served in many capacities in the church over the years. Recently, along with his wife, Shirley, he has led Sunday services at two assisted-living/memory-care facilities two times per month, along with leading Bible study sessions.